Rhyme?
And
Reason?

Lewis Carroll

Rhyme? And Reason?

Copyright © 2021 Bibliotech Press
All rights reserved

The present edition is a reproduction of previous publication of this classic work. Minor typographical errors may have been corrected without note; however, for an authentic reading experience the spelling, punctuation, and capitalization have been retained from the original text.

ISBN: 978-1-63637-428-4

CONTENTS

Phantasmagoria, in Seven Cantos:—

I The Trystyng	1
II Hys Fyve Rules	6
III Scarmoges	10
IV Hys Nouryture	14
V Byckerment	19
VI Dyscomfyture	24
VII Sad Souvenaunce	29
Echoes	31
A Sea Dirge	32
Ye Carpette Knyghte	34
Hiawatha's Photographing	35
Melancholetta	40
A Valentine	43

The Three Voices:

The First Voice	45
The Second Voice	50
The Third Voice	55
Tèma Con Variazióni	59
A Game of Fives	61
Poeta fit, non nascitur	62

The Hunting of the Snark, an Agony in Eight Fits:—	66
I The Landing	68
II The Bellman's Speech	72
III The Baker's Tale	76
IV The Hunting	79
V The Beaver's Lesson	82
VI The Barrister's Dream	87
VIII he Banker's Fate	90

VIII The Vanishing	92
Size and Tears	94
Atalanta in Camden Town	96
The Lang Coortin'	98
Four Riddles	104
Fame's Penny-Trumpet	110

Inscribed to a dear Child:
in memory of golden summer hours
and whispers of a summer sea.

Girt with a boyish garb for boyish task,
Eager she wields her spade: yet loves as well
Rest on a friendly knee, intent to ask
  The tale one loves to tell.

Rude scoffer of the seething outer strife,
Unmeet to read her pure and simple spright,
Deem, if thou wilt, such hours a waste of life,
  Empty of all delight!

Chat on, sweet Maid, and rescue from annoy
Hearts that by wiser talk are unbeguiled;
Ah, happy he who owns that tenderest joy,
  The heart-love of a child!

Away, fond thoughts, and vex my soul no more!
Work claims my wakeful nights, my busy days
Albeit bright memories of that sunlit shore
  Yet haunt my dreaming gaze!

[Of the following poems, Echoes, A Game of Fives, the last three of the Four Riddles, and Fame's Penny-Trumpet, are here published for the first time. The others have all appeared before, as have also the illustrations to The Hunting of the Snark.]

PHANTASMAGORIA

CANTO I

The Trystyng

One winter night, at half-past nine,
Cold, tired, and cross, and muddy,
I had come home, too late to dine,
And supper, with cigars and wine,
Was waiting in the study.

There was a strangeness in the room,
And Something white and wavy
Was standing near me in the gloom—
I took it for the carpet-broom
Left by that careless slavey.

But presently the Thing began
To shiver and to sneeze:
On which I said "Come, come, my man!
That's a most inconsiderate plan.
Less noise there, if you please!"

"I've caught a cold," the Thing replies,
"Out there upon the landing."
I turned to look in some surprise,
And there, before my very eyes,
A little Ghost was standing!

He trembled when he caught my eye,
And got behind a chair.
"How came you here," I said, "and why?
I never saw a thing so shy.
Come out! Don't shiver there!"

He said "I'd gladly tell you how,
And also tell you why;
But" (here he gave a little bow)
"You're in so bad a temper now,
You'd think it all a lie.

"And as to being in a fright,
Allow me to remark
That Ghosts have just as good a right,
In every way, to fear the light,
As Men to fear the dark."

"No plea," said I, "can well excuse
Such cowardice in you:
For Ghosts can visit when they choose,
Whereas we Humans ca'n't refuse
To grant the interview."

He said "A flutter of alarm
Is not unnatural, is it?
I really feared you meant some harm:
But, now I see that you are calm,
Let me explain my visit.

"Houses are classed, I beg to state,
According to the number
Of Ghosts that they accommodate:
(The Tenant merely counts as *weight*,
With Coals and other lumber).

"This is a 'one-ghost' house, and you
  When you arrived last summer,
May have remarked a Spectre who
Was doing all that Ghosts can do
  To welcome the new-comer.

"In Villas this is always done—
  However cheaply rented:
For, though of course there's less of fun
When there is only room for one,
  Ghosts have to be contented.

"That Spectre left you on the Third—
  Since then you've not been haunted:
For, as he never sent us word,
'Twas quite by accident we heard
  That any one was wanted.

"A Spectre has first choice, by right,
  In filling up a vacancy;
Then Phantom, Goblin, Elf, and Sprite—
If all these fail them, they invite
  The nicest Ghoul that they can see.

"The Spectres said the place was low,
  And that you kept bad wine:
So, as a Phantom had to go,
And I was first, of course, you know,
  I couldn't well decline."

"No doubt," said I, "they settled who
  Was fittest to be sent:
Yet still to choose a brat like you,
To haunt a man of forty-two,
  Was no great compliment!"

"I'm not so young, Sir," he replied,
"As you might think. The fact is,
In caverns by the water-side,
And other places that I've tried,
I've had a lot of practice:

"But I have never taken yet
A strict domestic part,
And in my flurry I forget
The Five Good Rules of Etiquette
We have to know by heart."

My sympathies were warming fast
Towards the little fellow:
He was so utterly aghast
At having found a Man at last,
And looked so scared and yellow.

"At least," I said, "I'm glad to find
A Ghost is not a dumb thing!
But pray sit down: you'll feel inclined
(If, like myself, you have not dined)
To take a snack of something:

"Though, certainly, you don't appear
A thing to offer food to!
And then I shall be glad to hear—
If you will say them loud and clear—
The Rules that you allude to."

"Thanks! You shall hear them by and by
This is a piece of luck!"
"What may I offer you?" said I.
"Well, since you are so kind, I'll try
A little bit of duck.

"One slice! And may I ask you for
Another drop of gravy?"
I sat and looked at him in awe,
For certainly I never saw
A thing so white and wavy.

And still he seemed to grow more white,
More vapoury, and wavier—
Seen in the dim and flickering light,
As he proceeded to recite
His "Maxims of Behaviour."

CANTO II

Hys Fyve Rules

"My First—but don't suppose," he said,
"I'm setting you a riddle—
Is—if your Victim be in bed,
Don't touch the curtains at his head,
But take them in the middle,

"And wave them slowly in and out,
While drawing them asunder;
And in a minute's time, no doubt,
He'll raise his head and look about
With eyes of wrath and wonder.

"And here you must on no pretence
Make the first observation.
Wait for the Victim to commence:
No Ghost of any common sense
Begins a conversation.

"If he should say *'How came you here?'*
(The way that you began, Sir,)
In such a case your course is clear—
'On the bat's back, my little dear!'
Is the appropriate answer.

"If after this he says no more,
You'd best perhaps curtail your
Exertions—go and shake the door,
And then, if he begins to snore,
You'll know the thing's a failure.

"By day, if he should be alone—
At home or on a walk—
You merely give a hollow groan,
To indicate the kind of tone
In which you mean to talk.

"But if you find him with his friends,
The thing is rather harder.
In such a case success depends
On picking up some candle-ends,
Or butter, in the larder.

"With this you make a kind of slide
(It answers best with suet),
On which you must contrive to glide,
And swing yourself from side to side—
One soon learns how to do it.

"The Second tells us what is right
In ceremonious calls:—
'First burn a blue or crimson light'
(A thing I quite forgot to-night),
'Then scratch the door or walls.'"

I said "You'll visit here no more,
If you attempt the Guy.
I'll have no bonfires on my floor—
And, as for scratching at the door,
I'd like to see you try!"

"The Third was written to protect
The interests of the Victim,
And tells us, as I recollect,
To treat him with a grave respect,
And not to contradict him."

7

"That's plain," said I, "as Tare and Tret,
　　To any comprehension:
I only wish *some* Ghosts I've met
　　Would not so *constantly* forget
　　The maxim that you mention!"

"Perhaps," he said, "you first transgressed
　　The laws of hospitality:
All Ghosts instinctively detest
The Man that fails to treat his guest
　　With proper cordiality.

"If you address a Ghost as 'Thing!'
　　Or strike him with a hatchet,
He is permitted by the King
To drop all formal parleying—
　　And then you're sure to catch it!

"The Fourth prohibits trespassing
　　Where other Ghosts are quartered:
And those convicted of the thing
(Unless when pardoned by the King)
　　Must instantly be slaughtered.

"That simply means 'be cut up small':
　　Ghosts soon unite anew:
The process scarcely hurts at all—
Not more than when *you're* what you call
　　'Cut up' by a Review.

"The Fifth is one you may prefer
　　That I should quote entire:—
The King must be addressed as 'Sir.'
This, from a simple courtier,
　　Is all the Laws require:

"But, should you wish to do the thing
With out-and-out politeness,
Accost him as 'My Goblin King!'
And always use, in answering,
The phrase 'Your Royal Whiteness!'

"I'm getting rather hoarse, I fear,
After so much reciting:
So, if you don't object, my dear,
We'll try a glass of bitter beer—
I think it looks inviting."

CANTO III

Scarmoges

"And did you really walk," said I,
"On such a wretched night?
I always fancied Ghosts could fly —
If not exactly in the sky,
Yet at a fairish height."

"It's very well," said he, "for Kings
To soar above the earth:
But Phantoms often find that wings —
Like many other pleasant things —
Cost more than they are worth.

"Spectres of course are rich, and so
Can buy them from the Elves:
But we prefer to keep below —
They're stupid company, you know.
For any but themselves:

"For, though they claim to be exempt
From pride, they treat a Phantom
As something quite beneath contempt —
Just as no Turkey ever dreamt
Of noticing a Bantam."

"They seem too proud," said I, "to go
To houses such as mine.
Pray, how did they contrive to know
So quickly that 'the place was low,'
And that I 'kept bad wine'?"

"Inspector Kobold came to you—"
The little Ghost began.
Here I broke in—"Inspector who?
Inspecting Ghosts is something new!
Explain yourself my man!"

"His name is Kobold," said my guest:
"One of the Spectre order:
You'll very often see him dressed
In a yellow gown, a crimson vest,
And a night-cap with a border.

"He tried the Brocken business first,
But caught a sort of chill;
So came to England to be nursed,
And here it took the form of *thirst*,
Which he complains of still.

"Port-wine, he says, when rich and sound,
Warms his old bones like nectar:
And as the inns, where it is found,
Are his especial hunting-ground,
We call him the *Inn-Spectre*."

I bore it—bore it like a man—
This agonizing witticism!
And nothing could be sweeter than
My temper, till the Ghost began
Some most provoking criticism.

"Cooks need not be indulged in waste;
Yet still you'd better teach them
Dishes should have *some sort* of taste.
Pray, why are all the cruets placed
Where nobody can reach them?

"That man of yours will never earn
　　His living as a waiter!
Is that queer *thing* supposed to burn?
　　(It's far too dismal a concern
　　　To call a Moderator).

"The duck was tender, but the peas
　　Were very much too old:
And just remember, if you please,
The next time you have toasted cheese,
　　Don't let them send it cold.

"You'd find the bread improved, I think,
　　By getting better flour:
And have you anything to drink
That looks a *little* less like ink,
　　And isn't *quite* so sour?"

Then, peering round with curious eyes,
　　He muttered "Goodness gracious!"
And so went on to criticise —
"Your room's an inconvenient size:
　　It's neither snug nor spacious.

"That narrow window, I expect,
　　Serves but to let the dusk in —"
"But please," said I, "to recollect
'Twas fashioned by an architect
　　Who pinned his faith on Ruskin!"

"I don't care who he was, Sir, or
　　On whom he pinned his faith!
Constructed by whatever law,
So poor a job I never saw,
　　As I'm a living Wraith!

"What a re-markable cigar!
How much are they a dozen?"
I growled "No matter what they are!
You're getting as familiar
As if you were my cousin!

"Now that's a thing *I will not stand*,
And so I tell you flat."
"Aha," said he, "we're getting grand!"
(Taking a bottle in his hand)
"I'll soon arrange *for that*!"

And here he took a careful aim,
And gaily cried "Here goes!"
I tried to dodge it as it came,
But somehow caught it, all the same,
Exactly on my nose.

And I remember nothing more
That I can clearly fix,
Till I was sitting on the floor,
Repeating "Two and five are four,
But *five and two* are six."

What really passed I never learned,
Nor guessed: I only know
That, when at last my sense returned,
The lamp, neglected, dimly burned —
The fire was getting low —

Through driving mists I seemed to see
A Thing that smirked and smiled:
And found that he was giving me
A lesson in Biography,
As if I were a child.

CANTO IV

Hys Nouryture

"Oh, when I was a little Ghost,
　A merry time had we!
Each seated on his favourite post,
We chumped and chawed the buttered toast
　They gave us for our tea."

"That story is in print!" I cried.
　"Don't say it's not, because
It's known as well as Bradshaw's Guide!"
　(The Ghost uneasily replied
　He hardly thought it was).

"It's not in Nursery Rhymes? And yet
　I almost think it is—
'Three little Ghosteses' were set
'On posteses,' you know, and ate
　Their 'buttered toasteses.'

"I have the book; so, if you doubt it—"
　I turned to search the shelf.
"Don't stir!" he cried. "We'll do without it;
I now remember all about it;
　I wrote the thing myself.

"It came out in a 'Monthly,' or
　At least my agent said it did:
Some literary swell, who saw
It, thought it seemed adapted for
　The Magazine he edited.

"My father was a Brownie, Sir;
My mother was a Fairy.
The notion had occurred to her,
The children would be happier,
If they were taught to vary.

"The notion soon became a craze;
And, when it once began, she
Brought us all out in different ways—
One was a Pixy, two were Fays,
Another was a Banshee;

"The Fetch and Kelpie went to school,
And gave a lot of trouble;
Next came a Poltergeist and Ghoul,
And then two Trolls (which broke the rule),
A Goblin, and a Double—

"(If that's a snuff-box on the shelf,"
He added with a yawn,
"I'll take a pinch)—next came an Elf,
And then a Phantom (that's myself),
And last, a Leprechaun.

"One day, some Spectres chanced to call,
Dressed in the usual white:
I stood and watched them in the hall,
And couldn't make them out at all,
They seemed so strange a sight.

"I wondered what on earth they were,
That looked all head and sack;
But Mother told me not to stare,
And then she twitched me by the hair,
And punched me in the back.

"Since then I've often wished that I
Had been a Spectre born.
But what's the use?" (He heaved a sigh).
"*They* are the ghost-nobility,
And look on us with scorn.

"My phantom-life was soon begun:
When I was barely six,
I went out with an older one—
And just at first I thought it fun,
And learned a lot of tricks.

"I've haunted dungeons, castles, towers—
Wherever I was sent:
I've often sat and howled for hours,
Drenched to the skin with driving showers,
Upon a battlement.

"It's quite old-fashioned now to groan
When you begin to speak:
This is the newest thing in tone—"
And here (it chilled me to the bone)
He gave an *awful* squeak.

"Perhaps," he added, "to *your* ear
That sounds an easy thing?
Try it yourself, my little dear!
It took me something like a year,
With constant practising.

"And when you've learned to squeak, my man,
And caught the double sob,
You're pretty much where you began:
Just try and gibber if you can!
That's something *like* a job!

"I've tried it, and can only say
I'm sure you couldn't do it, e-
ven if you practised night and day,
Unless you have a turn that way,
And natural ingenuity.

"Shakspeare I think it is who treats
Of Ghosts, in days of old,
Who 'gibbered in the Roman streets,'
Dressed, if you recollect, in sheets—
They must have found it cold.

"I've often spent ten pounds on stuff,
In dressing as a Double;
But, though it answers as a puff,
It never has effect enough
To make it worth the trouble.

"Long bills soon quenched the little thirst
I had for being funny.
The setting-up is always worst:
Such heaps of things you want at first,
One must be made of money!

"For instance, take a Haunted Tower,
With skull, cross-bones, and sheet;
Blue lights to burn (say) two an hour,
Condensing lens of extra power,
And set of chains complete:

"What with the things you have to hire—
The fitting on the robe—
And testing all the coloured fire—
The outfit of itself would tire
The patience of a Job!

"And then they're so fastidious,
The Haunted-House Committee:
I've often known them make a fuss
Because a Ghost was French, or Russ,
Or even from the City!

"Some dialects are objected to—
For one, the Irish brogue is:
And then, for all you have to do,
One pound a week they offer you,
And find yourself in Bogies!"

CANTO V

Byckerment

"Don't they consult the 'Victims,' though?"
I said. "They should, by rights,
Give them a chance—because, you know,
The tastes of people differ so,
Especially in Sprites."

The Phantom shook his head and smiled.
"Consult them? Not a bit!
'Twould be a job to drive one wild,
To satisfy one single child—
There'd be no end to it!"

"Of course you can't leave *children* free,"
Said I, "to pick and choose:
But, in the case of men like me,
I think 'Mine Host' might fairly be
Allowed to state his views."

He said "It really wouldn't pay—
Folk are so full of fancies.
We visit for a single day,
And whether then we go, or stay,
Depends on circumstances.

"And, though we don't consult 'Mine Host'
Before the thing's arranged,
Still, if he often quits his post,
Or is not a well-mannered Ghost,
Then you can have him changed.

"But if the host's a man like you—
I mean a man of sense;
And if the house is not too new—"
"Why, what has that," said I, "to do
With Ghost's convenience?"

"A new house does not suit, you know—
It's such a job to trim it:
But, after twenty years or so,
The wainscotings begin to go,
So twenty is the limit."

"To trim" was not a phrase I could
Remember having heard:
"Perhaps," I said, "you'll be so good
As tell me what is understood
Exactly by that word?"

"It means the loosening all the doors,"
The Ghost replied, and laughed:
"It means the drilling holes by scores
In all the skirting-boards and floors,
To make a thorough draught.

"You'll sometimes find that one or two
Are all you really need
To let the wind come whistling through—
But here there'll be a lot to do!"
I faintly gasped "Indeed!

"If I'd been rather later, I'll
Be bound," I added, trying
(Most unsuccessfully) to smile,
"You'd have been busy all this while,
Trimming and beautifying?"

"Why, no," said he; "perhaps I should
　　Have stayed another minute—
But still no Ghost, that's any good,
Without an introduction would
　　Have ventured to begin it.

"The proper thing, as you were late,
　　Was certainly to go:
But, with the roads in such a state,
I got the Knight-Mayor's leave to wait
　　For half an hour or so."

"Who's the Knight-Mayor?" I cried. Instead
　　Of answering my question,
"Well! If you don't know that," he said,
"Either you never go to bed,
　　Or you've a grand digestion!

"He goes about and sits on folk
　　That eat too much at night:
His duties are to pinch, and poke,
And squeeze them till they nearly choke."
　　(I said "It serves them right!")

"And folk that sup on things like these—"
　　He muttered, "eggs and bacon—
Lobster—and duck—and toasted cheese—
If they don't get an awful squeeze,
　　I'm very much mistaken!

"He is immensely fat, and so
　　Well suits the occupation:
In point of fact, if you must know,
We used to call him, years ago,
　　The Mayor and Corporation!

"The day he was elected Mayor
I *know* that every Sprite meant
To vote for *me*, but did not dare—
He was so frantic with despair
And furious with excitement.

"When it was over, for a whim,
He ran to tell the King;
And being the reverse of slim,
A two-mile trot was not for him
A very easy thing.

"So, to reward him for his run
(As it was baking hot,
And he was over twenty stone),
The King proceeded, half in fun,
To knight him on the spot."

"'Twas a great liberty to take!"
(I fired up like a rocket).
"He did it just for punning's sake:
'The man,' says Johnson, 'that would make
A pun, would pick a pocket!'"

"A man," said he, "is not a King."
I argued for a while,
And did my best to prove the thing—
The Phantom merely listening
With a contemptuous smile.

At last, when, breath and patience spent,
I had recourse to smoking—
"Your *aim*," he said, "is excellent:
But—when you call it *argument*—
Of course you're only joking?"

Stung by his cold and snaky eye,
I roused myself at length
To say "At least I do defy
The veriest sceptic to deny
That union is strength!"

"That's true enough," said he, "yet stay—"
I listened in all meekness—
"Union is strength, I'm bound to say;
In fact, the thing's as clear as day;
But *onions*—are a weakness."

CANTO VI

Dyscomfyture

As one who strives a hill to climb,
　Who never climbed before:
　Who finds it, in a little time,
　Grow every moment less sublime,
And votes the thing a bore:

Yet, having once begun to try,
　Dares not desert his quest,
　But, climbing, ever keeps his eye
　On one small hut against the sky,
Wherein he hopes to rest:

Who climbs till nerve and force are spent,
　With many a puff and pant:
　Who still, as rises the ascent,
　In language grows more violent,
Although in breath more scant:

Who, climbing, gains at length the place
　That crowns the upward track;
　And, entering with unsteady pace,
　Receives a buffet in the face
That lands him on his back:

And feels himself, like one in sleep,
　Glide swiftly down again,
A helpless weight, from steep to steep,
　Till, with a headlong giddy sweep,
　He drops upon the plain—

So I, that had resolved to bring
    Conviction to a ghost,
And found it quite a different thing
    From any human arguing,
    Yet dared not quit my post

But, keeping still the end in view
    To which I hoped to come,
I strove to prove the matter true
    By putting everything I knew
    Into an axiom:

Commencing every single phrase
    With 'therefore' or 'because,'
I blindly reeled, a hundred ways,
    About the syllogistic maze,
    Unconscious where I was.

Quoth he "That's regular clap-trap:
    Don't bluster any more.
Now do be cool and take a nap!
    Such a ridiculous old chap
    Was never seen before!

"You're like a man I used to meet,
    Who got one day so furious
    In arguing, the simple heat
Scorched both his slippers off his feet!"
    I said *"That's very curious!"*

"Well, it is curious, I agree,
    And sounds perhaps like fibs:
But still it's true as true can be—
As sure as your name's Tibbs," said he.
    I said "My name's not Tibbs."

"Not Tibbs!" he cried—his tone became
A shade or two less hearty—
"Why, no," said I. "My proper name
Is Tibbets—" "Tibbets?" "Aye, the same."
"Why, then YOU'RE NOT THE PARTY!"

With that he struck the board a blow
That shivered half the glasses.
"Why couldn't you have told me so
Three quarters of an hour ago,
You prince of all the asses?

"To walk four miles through mud and rain,
To spend the night in smoking,
And then to find that it's in vain—
And I've to do it all again—
It's really too provoking!

"Don't talk!" he cried, as I began
To mutter some excuse.
"Who can have patience with a man
That's got no more discretion than
An idiotic goose?

"To keep me waiting here, instead
Of telling me at once
That this was not the house!" he said.
"There, that'll do—be off to bed!
Don't gape like that, you dunce!"

"It's very fine to throw the blame
On me in such a fashion!
Why didn't you enquire my name
The very minute that you came?"
I answered in a passion.

"Of course it worries you a bit
To come so far on foot—
But how was I to blame for it?"
"Well, well!" said he. "I must admit
That isn't badly put.

"And certainly you've given me
The best of wine and victual—
Excuse my violence," said he,
"But accidents like this, you see,
They put one out a little.

"'Twas my fault after all, I find—
Shake hands, old Turnip-top!"
The name was hardly to my mind,
But, as no doubt he meant it kind,
I let the matter drop.

"Good-night, old Turnip-top, good-night!
When I am gone, perhaps
They'll send you some inferior Sprite,
Who'll keep you in a constant fright
And spoil your soundest naps.

"Tell him you'll stand no sort of trick;
Then, if he leers and chuckles,
You just be handy with a stick
(Mind that it's pretty hard and thick)
And rap him on the knuckles!

"Then carelessly remark 'Old coon!
Perhaps you're not aware
That, if you don't behave, you'll soon
Be chuckling to another tune—
And so you'd best take care!'

"That's the right way to cure a Sprite
Of such-like goings-on—
But gracious me! It's getting light!
Good-night, old Turnip-top, good-night!"
A nod, and he was gone.

CANTO VII

Sad Souvenaunce

"What's this?" I pondered. "Have I slept?
Or can I have been drinking?"
But soon a gentler feeling crept
Upon me, and I sat and wept
An hour or so, like winking.

"No need for Bones to hurry so!"
I sobbed. "In fact, I doubt
If it was worth his while to go—
And who is Tibbs, I'd like to know,
To make such work about?

"If Tibbs is anything like me,
It's *possible*," I said,
"He won't be over-pleased to be
Dropped in upon at half-past three,
After he's snug in bed.

"And if Bones plagues him anyhow—
Squeaking and all the rest of it,
As he was doing here just now—
I prophesy there'll be a row,
And Tibbs will have the best of it!"

Then, as my tears could never bring
The friendly Phantom back,
It seemed to me the proper thing
To mix another glass, and sing
The following Coronach.

'And art thou gone, beloved Ghost?
Best of Familiars!
Nay then, farewell, my duckling roast,
Farewell, farewell, my tea and toast,
My meerschaum and cigars!

'The hues of life are dull and gray,
The sweets of life insipid,
When thou, my charmer, art away—
Old Brick, or rather, let me say,
Old Parallelepiped!'

Instead of singing Verse the Third,
I ceased—abruptly, rather:
But, after such a splendid word,
I felt that it would be absurd
To try it any farther.

So with a yawn I went my way
To seek the welcome downy,
And slept, and dreamed till break of day
Of Poltergeist and Fetch and Fay
And Leprechaun and Brownie!

For years I've not been visited
By any kind of Sprite;
Yet still they echo in my head,
Those parting words, so kindly said,
"Old Turnip-top, good-night!"

ECHOES

          Lady Clara Vere de Vere
         Was eight years old, she said:
Every ringlet, lightly shaken, ran itself in golden thread.

          She took her little porringer:
        Of me she shall not win renown:
For the baseness of its nature shall have strength to drag her down.

       "Sisters and brothers, little Maid?
     There stands the Inspector at thy door:
Like a dog, he hunts for boys who know not two and two are four."

       "Kind words are more than coronets,"
     She said, and wondering looked at me:
"It is the dead unhappy night, and I must hurry home to tea."

A SEA DIRGE

There are certain things—as, a spider, a ghost,
The income-tax, gout, an umbrella for three—
That I hate, but the thing that I hate the most
    Is a thing they call the Sea.

Pour some salt water over the floor—
Ugly I'm sure you'll allow it to be:
Suppose it extended a mile or more,
    That's very like the Sea.

Beat a dog till it howls outright—
Cruel, but all very well for a spree:
Suppose that he did so day and night,
    That would be like the Sea.

I had a vision of nursery-maids;
Tens of thousands passed by me—
All leading children with wooden spades,
    And this was by the Sea.

Who invented those spades of wood?
Who was it cut them out of the tree?
None, I think, but an idiot could—
    Or one that loved the Sea.

It is pleasant and dreamy, no doubt, to float
With 'thoughts as boundless, and souls as free':
But, suppose you are very unwell in the boat,
    How do you like the Sea?

There is an insect that people avoid
(Whence is derived the verb 'to flee').
Where have you been by it most annoyed?
    In lodgings by the Sea.

If you like your coffee with sand for dregs,
    A decided hint of salt in your tea,
And a fishy taste in the very eggs—
    By all means choose the Sea.

And if, with these dainties to drink and eat,
    You prefer not a vestige of grass or tree,
And a chronic state of wet in your feet,
    Then—I recommend the Sea.

For I have friends who dwell by the coast—
    Pleasant friends they are to me!
It is when I am with them I wonder most
    That any one likes the Sea.

They take me a walk: though tired and stiff,
    To climb the heights I madly agree;
And, after a tumble or so from the cliff,
    They kindly suggest the Sea.

I try the rocks, and I think it cool
    That they laugh with such an excess of glee,
As I heavily slip into every pool
    That skirts the cold cold Sea.

YE CARPETTE KNYGHTE

I have a horse—a ryghte goode horse—
Ne doe I envye those
Who scoure ye playne yn headye course
Tyll soddayne on theyre nose
They lyghte wyth unexpected force—
Yt ys—a horse of clothes.

I have a saddel—"Say'st thou soe?
Wyth styrruppes, Knyghte, to boote?"
I sayde not that—I answere "Noe"—
Yt lacketh such, I woote:
Yt ys a mutton-saddel, loe!
Parte of ye fleecye brute.

I have a bytte—a ryghte good bytte—
As shall bee seene yn tyme.
Ye jawe of horse yt wyll not fytte;
Yts use ys more sublyme.
Fayre Syr, how deemest thou of yt?
Yt ys—thys bytte of rhyme.

HIAWATHA'S PHOTOGRAPHING

[In an age of imitation, I can claim no special merit for this slight attempt at doing what is known to be so easy. Any fairly practised writer, with the slightest ear for rhythm, could compose, for hours together, in the easy running metre of 'The Song of Hiawatha.' Having, then, distinctly stated that I challenge no attention in the following little poem to its merely verbal jingle, I must beg the candid reader to confine his criticism to its treatment of the subject.]

From his shoulder Hiawatha
Took the camera of rosewood,
Made of sliding, folding rosewood;
Neatly put it all together.
In its case it lay compactly,
Folded into nearly nothing;
But he opened out the hinges,
Pushed and pulled the joints and hinges,
Till it looked all squares and oblongs,
Like a complicated figure
In the Second Book of Euclid.

This he perched upon a tripod—
Crouched beneath its dusky cover—
Stretched his hand, enforcing silence—
Said "Be motionless, I beg you!"
Mystic, awful was the process.
All the family in order
Sat before him for their pictures:
Each in turn, as he was taken,
Volunteered his own suggestions,
His ingenious suggestions.
First the Governor, the Father:
He suggested velvet curtains

Looped about a massy pillar;
And the corner of a table,
Of a rosewood dining-table.
He would hold a scroll of something,
Hold it firmly in his left-hand;
He would keep his right-hand buried
(Like Napoleon) in his waistcoat;
He would contemplate the distance
With a look of pensive meaning,
As of ducks that die in tempests.
Grand, heroic was the notion:
Yet the picture failed entirely:
Failed, because he moved a little,
Moved, because he couldn't help it.
Next, his better half took courage;
She would have her picture taken.
She came dressed beyond description,
Dressed in jewels and in satin
Far too gorgeous for an empress.

Gracefully she sat down sideways,
With a simper scarcely human,
Holding in her hand a bouquet
Rather larger than a cabbage.
All the while that she was sitting,
Still the lady chattered, chattered,
Like a monkey in the forest.
"Am I sitting still?" she asked him.
"Is my face enough in profile?
Shall I hold the bouquet higher?
Will it come into the picture?"
And the picture failed completely.
Next the Son, the Stunning-Cantab:
He suggested curves of beauty,
Curves pervading all his figure,
Which the eye might follow onward,

Till they centered in the breast-pin,
Centered in the golden breast-pin.
He had learnt it all from Ruskin
(Author of 'The Stones of Venice,'
'Seven Lamps of Architecture,'
'Modern Painters,' and some others);
And perhaps he had not fully
Understood his author's meaning;
But, whatever was the reason,
All was fruitless, as the picture
Ended in an utter failure.

Next to him the eldest daughter:
She suggested very little,
Only asked if he would take her
With her look of 'passive beauty.'
Her idea of passive beauty
Was a squinting of the left-eye,
Was a drooping of the right-eye,
Was a smile that went up sideways
To the corner of the nostrils.
Hiawatha, when she asked him,
Took no notice of the question,
Looked as if he hadn't heard it;
But, when pointedly appealed to,
Smiled in his peculiar manner,
Coughed and said it 'didn't matter,'
Bit his lip and changed the subject.
Nor in this was he mistaken,
As the picture failed completely.
So in turn the other sisters.

Last, the youngest son was taken:
Very rough and thick his hair was,
Very round and red his face was,
Very dusty was his jacket,

Very fidgety his manner.
And his overbearing sisters
Called him names he disapproved of:
Called him Johnny, 'Daddy's Darling,'
Called him Jacky, 'Scrubby School-boy.'
And, so awful was the picture,
In comparison the others
Seemed, to one's bewildered fancy,
To have partially succeeded.
Finally my Hiawatha
Tumbled all the tribe together,
('Grouped' is not the right expression),
And, as happy chance would have it,
Did at last obtain a picture
Where the faces all succeeded:
Each came out a perfect likeness.

Then they joined and all abused it,
Unrestrainedly abused it,
As the worst and ugliest picture
They could possibly have dreamed of.
Giving one such strange expressions—
Sullen, stupid, pert expressions.
Really any one would take us
(Any one that did not know us)
For the most unpleasant people!'
(Hiawatha seemed to think so,
Seemed to think it not unlikely).
All together rang their voices,
Angry, loud, discordant voices,
As of dogs that howl in concert,
As of cats that wail in chorus.
But my Hiawatha's patience,
His politeness and his patience,
Unaccountably had vanished,
And he left that happy party.

Neither did he leave them slowly,
With the calm deliberation,
The intense deliberation
Of a photographic artist:
But he left them in a hurry,
Left them in a mighty hurry,
Stating that he would not stand it,
Stating in emphatic language
What he'd be before he'd stand it.
Hurriedly he packed his boxes:
Hurriedly the porter trundled
On a barrow all his boxes:
Hurriedly he took his ticket:
Hurriedly the train received him:
Thus departed Hiawatha.

MELANCHOLETTA

With saddest music all day long
She soothed her secret sorrow:
At night she sighed "I fear 'twas wrong
Such cheerful words to borrow.
Dearest, a sweeter, sadder song
I'll sing to thee to-morrow."

I thanked her, but I could not say
That I was glad to hear it:
I left the house at break of day,
And did not venture near it
Till time, I hoped, had worn away
Her grief, for nought could cheer it!

My dismal sister! Couldst thou know
The wretched home thou keepest!
Thy brother, drowned in daily woe,
Is thankful when thou sleepest;
For if I laugh, however low,
When thou'rt awake, thou weepest!

I took my sister t'other day
(Excuse the slang expression)
To Sadler's Wells to see the play,
In hopes the new impression
Might in her thoughts, from grave to gay
Effect some slight digression.

I asked three gay young dogs from town
To join us in our folly,
Whose mirth, I thought, might serve to drown
My sister's melancholy:
The lively Jones, the sportive Brown,
And Robinson the jolly.

The maid announced the meal in tones
  That I myself had taught her,
Meant to allay my sister's moans
  Like oil on troubled water:
I rushed to Jones, the lively Jones,
  And begged him to escort her.

Vainly he strove, with ready wit,
  To joke about the weather—
To ventilate the last '*on dit*'—
  To quote the price of leather—
She groaned "Here I and Sorrow sit:
  Let us lament together!"

I urged "You're wasting time, you know:
  Delay will spoil the venison."
"My heart is wasted with my woe!
  There is no rest—in Venice, on
The Bridge of Sighs!" she quoted low
  From Byron and from Tennyson.

I need not tell of soup and fish
  In solemn silence swallowed,
The sobs that ushered in each dish,
  And its departure followed,
Nor yet my suicidal wish
  To *be* the cheese I hollowed.

Some desperate attempts were made
  To start a conversation;
"Madam," the sportive Brown essayed,
  "Which kind of recreation,
Hunting or fishing, have you made
  Your special occupation?"

Her lips curved downwards instantly,
As if of india-rubber.
"Hounds *in full cry* I like," said she:
(Oh how I longed to snub her!)
"Of fish, a whale's the one for me,
It is so full of blubber!"

The night's performance was "King John."
"It's dull," she wept, "and so-so!"
A while I let her tears flow on,
She said they soothed her woe so!
At length the curtain rose upon
'Bombastes Furioso.'

In vain we roared; in vain we tried
To rouse her into laughter:
Her pensive glances wandered wide
From orchestra to rafter—
"*Tier upon tier!*" she said, and sighed;
And silence followed after.

A VALENTINE

[Sent to a friend who had complained that I was glad enough to see him when he came, but didn't seem to miss him if he stayed away.]

>And cannot pleasures, while they last,
>Be actual unless, when past,
>They leave us shuddering and aghast,
>   With anguish smarting?
>And cannot friends be firm and fast,
>   And yet bear parting?
>
>And must I then, at Friendship's call,
>Calmly resign the little all
>(Trifling, I grant, it is and small)
>   I have of gladness,
>And lend my being to the thrall
>   Of gloom and sadness?
>
>And think you that I should be dumb,
>And full *dolorum omnium*,
>*Excepting* when *you* choose to come
>   And share my dinner?
>At other times be sour and glum
>   And daily thinner?
>
>Must he then only live to weep,
>Who'd prove his friendship true and deep?
>By day a lonely shadow creep,
>   At night-time languish,
>Oft raising in his broken sleep
>   The moan of anguish?
>
>The lover, if for certain days

His fair one be denied his gaze,
Sinks not in grief and wild amaze,
    But, wiser wooer,
He spends the time in writing lays,
    And posts them to her.

And if the verse flow free and fast,
Till even the poet is aghast,
A touching Valentine at last
    The post shall carry,
When thirteen days are gone and past
    Of February.

Farewell, dear friend, and when we meet,
In desert waste or crowded street,
Perhaps before this week shall fleet,
    Perhaps to-morrow,
I trust to find *your* heart the seat
    Of wasting sorrow.

THE THREE VOICES

The First Voice

He trilled a carol fresh and free:
He laughed aloud for very glee:
There came a breeze from off the sea:

It passed athwart the glooming flat—
It fanned his forehead as he sat—
It lightly bore away his hat,

All to the feet of one who stood
Like maid enchanted in a wood,
Frowning as darkly as she could.

With huge umbrella, lank and brown,
Unerringly she pinned it down,
Right through the centre of the crown.

Then, with an aspect cold and grim,
Regardless of its battered rim,
She took it up and gave it him.

A while like one in dreams he stood,
Then faltered forth his gratitude
In words just short of being rude:

For it had lost its shape and shine,
And it had cost him four-and-nine,
And he was going out to dine.

"To dine!" she sneered in acid tone.
"To bend thy being to a bone
Clothed in a radiance not its own!"

The tear-drop trickled to his chin:
There was a meaning in her grin
That made him feel on fire within.

"Term it not 'radiance,'" said he:
"'Tis solid nutriment to me.
Dinner is Dinner: Tea is Tea."

And she "Yea so? Yet wherefore cease?
Let thy scant knowledge find increase.
Say 'Men are Men, and Geese are Geese.'"

He moaned: he knew not what to say.
The thought "That I could get away!"
Strove with the thought "But I must stay."

"To dine!" she shrieked in dragon-wrath.
"To swallow wines all foam and froth!
To simper at a table-cloth!

"Say, can thy noble spirit stoop
To join the gormandising troop
Who find a solace in the soup?

"Canst thou desire or pie or puff?
Thy well-bred manners were enough,
Without such gross material stuff."

"Yet well-bred men," he faintly said,
"Are not unwilling to be fed:
Nor are they well without the bread."

Her visage scorched him ere she spoke:
"There are," she said, "a kind of folk
Who have no horror of a joke.

"Such wretches live: they take their share
Of common earth and common air:
We come across them here and there:

"We grant them—there is no escape—
A sort of semi-human shape
Suggestive of the man-like Ape."

"In all such theories," said he,
"One fixed exception there must be.
That is, the Present Company."

Baffled, she gave a wolfish bark:
He, aiming blindly in the dark,
With random shaft had pierced the mark.

She felt that her defeat was plain,
Yet madly strove with might and main
To get the upper hand again.

Fixing her eyes upon the beach,
As though unconscious of his speech,
She said "Each gives to more than each."

He could not answer yea or nay:
He faltered "Gifts may pass away."
Yet knew not what he meant to say.

"If that be so," she straight replied,
"Each heart with each doth coincide.
What boots it? For the world is wide."

"The world is but a Thought," said he:
"The vast unfathomable sea
Is but a Notion—unto me."

And darkly fell her answer dread
Upon his unresisting head,
Like half a hundredweight of lead.

"The Good and Great must ever shun
That reckless and abandoned one
Who stoops to perpetrate a pun.

"The man that smokes—that reads the Times—
That goes to Christmas Pantomimes—
Is capable of any crimes!"

He felt it was his turn to speak,
And, with a shamed and crimson cheek,
Moaned "This is harder than Bezique!"

But when she asked him "Wherefore so?"
He felt his very whiskers glow,
And frankly owned "I do not know."

While, like broad waves of golden grain,
Or sunlit hues on cloistered pane,
His colour came and went again.

Pitying his obvious distress,
Yet with a tinge of bitterness,
She said "The More exceeds the Less."

"A truth of such undoubted weight,"
He urged, "and so extreme in date,
It were superfluous to state."

Roused into sudden passion, she
In tone of cold malignity:
"To others, yea: but not to thee."

But when she saw him quail and quake,
And when he urged "For pity's sake!"
Once more in gentle tone she spake.

"Thought in the mind doth still abide:
That is by Intellect supplied,
And within that Idea doth hide:

"And he, that yearns the truth to know,
Still further inwardly may go,
And find Idea from Notion flow:

"And thus the chain, that sages sought,
Is to a glorious circle wrought,
For Notion hath its source in Thought."

So passed they on with even pace:
Yet gradually one might trace
A shadow growing on his face.

The Second Voice

They walked beside the wave-worn beach;
Her tongue was very apt to teach,
And now and then he did beseech

She would abate her dulcet tone,
Because the talk was all her own,
And he was dull as any drone.

She urged "No cheese is made of chalk":
And ceaseless flowed her dreary talk,
Tuned to the footfall of a walk.

Her voice was very full and rich,
And, when at length she asked him "Which?"
It mounted to its highest pitch.

He a bewildered answer gave,
Drowned in the sullen moaning wave,
Lost in the echoes of the cave.

He answered her he knew not what:
Like shaft from bow at random shot,
He spoke, but she regarded not.

She waited not for his reply,
But with a downward leaden eye
Went on as if he were not by:

Sound argument and grave defence,
Strange questions raised on "Why?" and "Whence?"
And wildly tangled evidence.

When he, with racked and whirling brain,
Feebly implored her to explain,
She simply said it all again.

Wrenched with an agony intense,
He spake, neglecting Sound and Sense,
And careless of all consequence:

"Mind—I believe—is Essence—Ent—
Abstract—that is—an Accident—
Which we—that is to say—I meant—"

When, with quick breath and cheeks all flushed,
At length his speech was somewhat hushed,
She looked at him, and he was crushed.

It needed not her calm reply:
She fixed him with a stony eye,
And he could neither fight nor fly,

While she dissected, word by word,
His speech, half guessed at and half heard,
As might a cat a little bird.

Then, having wholly overthrown
His views, and stripped them to the bone,
Proceeded to unfold her own.

"Shall Man be Man? And shall he miss
Of other thoughts no thought but this,
Harmonious dews of sober bliss?

"What boots it? Shall his fevered eye
Through towering nothingness descry
The grisly phantom hurry by?

"And hear dumb shrieks that fill the air;
See mouths that gape, and eyes that stare
And redden in the dusky glare?

"The meadows breathing amber light,
The darkness toppling from the height,
The feathery train of granite Night?

"Shall he, grown gray among his peers,
Through the thick curtain of his tears
Catch glimpses of his earlier years,

"And hear the sounds he knew of yore,
Old shufflings on the sanded floor,
Old knuckles tapping at the door?

"Yet still before him as he flies
One pallid form shall ever rise,
And, bodying forth in glassy eyes

"The vision of a vanished good,
Low peering through the tangled wood,
Shall freeze the current of his blood."

Still from each fact, with skill uncouth
And savage rapture, like a tooth
She wrenched some slow reluctant truth.

Till, like a silent water-mill,
When summer suns have dried the rill,
She reached a full stop, and was still.

Dead calm succeeded to the fuss,
As when the loaded omnibus
Has reached the railway terminus:

When, for the tumult of the street,
Is heard the engine's stifled beat,
The velvet tread of porters' feet.

With glance that ever sought the ground,
She moved her lips without a sound,
And every now and then she frowned.

He gazed upon the sleeping sea,
And joyed in its tranquillity,
And in that silence dead, but she

To muse a little space did seem,
Then, like the echo of a dream,
Harped back upon her threadbare theme.

Still an attentive ear he lent
But could not fathom what she meant:
She was not deep, nor eloquent.

He marked the ripple on the sand:
The even swaying of her hand
Was all that he could understand.

He saw in dreams a drawing-room,
Where thirteen wretches sat in gloom,
Waiting — he thought he knew for whom:

He saw them drooping here and there,
Each feebly huddled on a chair,
In attitudes of blank despair:

Oysters were not more mute than they,
For all their brains were pumped away,
And they had nothing more to say —

Save one, who groaned "Three hours are gone!"
Who shrieked "We'll wait no longer, John!
Tell them to set the dinner on!"

The vision passed: the ghosts were fled:
He saw once more that woman dread:
He heard once more the words she said.

He left her, and he turned aside:
He sat and watched the coming tide
Across the shores so newly dried.

He wondered at the waters clear,
The breeze that whispered in his ear,
The billows heaving far and near,

And why he had so long preferred
To hang upon her every word:
"In truth," he said, "it was absurd."

The Third Voice

Not long this transport held its place:
Within a little moment's space
Quick tears were raining down his face.

His heart stood still, aghast with fear;
A wordless voice, nor far nor near,
He seemed to hear and not to hear.

"Tears kindle not the doubtful spark.
If so, why not? Of this remark
The bearings are profoundly dark."

"Her speech," he said, "hath caused this pain.
Easier I count it to explain
The jargon of the howling main,

"Or, stretched beside some babbling brook,
To con, with inexpressive look,
An unintelligible book."

Low spake the voice within his head,
In words imagined more than said,
Soundless as ghost's intended tread:

"If thou art duller than before,
Why quittedst thou the voice of lore?
Why not endure, expecting more?"

"Rather than that," he groaned aghast,
"I'd writhe in depths of cavern vast,
Some loathly vampire's rich repast."

"'Twere hard," it answered, "themes immense
To coop within the narrow fence
That rings thy scant intelligence."

"Not so," he urged, "nor once alone:
But there was something in her tone
That chilled me to the very bone.

"Her style was anything but clear,
And most unpleasantly severe;
Her epithets were very queer.

"And yet, so grand were her replies,
I could not choose but deem her wise;
I did not dare to criticise;

"Nor did I leave her, till she went
So deep in tangled argument
That all my powers of thought were spent."

A little whisper inly slid,
"Yet truth is truth: you know you did."
A little wink beneath the lid.

And, sickened with excess of dread,
Prone to the dust he bent his head,
And lay like one three-quarters dead.

The whisper left him—like a breeze
Lost in the depths of leafy trees—
Left him by no means at his ease.

Once more he weltered in despair,
With hands, through denser-matted hair,
More tightly clenched than then they were.

When, bathed in Dawn of living red,
Majestic frowned the mountain head,
"Tell me my fault," was all he said.

When, at high Noon, the blazing sky
Scorched in his head each haggard eye,
Then keenest rose his weary cry.

And when at Eve the unpitying sun
Smiled grimly on the solemn fun,
"Alack," he sighed, "what have I done?"

But saddest, darkest was the sight,
When the cold grasp of leaden Night
Dashed him to earth, and held him tight.

Tortured, unaided, and alone,
Thunders were silence to his groan,
Bagpipes sweet music to its tone:

"What? Ever thus, in dismal round,
Shall Pain and Mystery profound
Pursue me like a sleepless hound,

"With crimson-dashed and eager jaws,
Me, still in ignorance of the cause,
Unknowing what I broke of laws?"

The whisper to his ear did seem
Like echoed flow of silent stream,
Or shadow of forgotten dream,

The whisper trembling in the wind:
"Her fate with thine was intertwined,"
So spake it in his inner mind:

"Each orbed on each a baleful star:
Each proved the other's blight and bar:
Each unto each were best, most far:

"Yea, each to each was worse than foe:
Thou, a scared dullard, gibbering low,
And she, an avalanche of woe!"

TÈMA CON VARIAZIÓNI

[Why is it that Poetry has never yet been subjected to that process of Dilution which has proved so advantageous to her sister-art Music? The Diluter gives us first a few notes of some well-known Air, then a dozen bars of his own, then a few more notes of the Air, and so on alternately: thus saving the listener, if not from all risk of recognising the melody at all, at least from the too-exciting transports which it might produce in a more concentrated form. The process is termed "setting" by Composers, and any one, that has ever experienced the emotion of being unexpectedly set down in a heap of mortar, will recognise the truthfulness of this happy phrase.
For truly, just as the genuine Epicure lingers lovingly over a morsel of supreme Venison—whose every fibre seems to murmur "Excelsior!"—yet swallows, ere returning to the toothsome dainty, great mouthfuls of oatmeal-porridge and winkles: and just as the perfect Connoisseur in Claret permits himself but one delicate sip, and then tosses off a pint or more of boarding-school beer: so also—

I never loved a dear Gazelle—
Nor anything that cost me much:
High prices profit those who sell,
But why should I be fond of such?

To glad me with his soft black eye
My son comes trotting home from school;
He's had a fight, but can't tell why—
He always was a little fool!

But, when he came to know me well,
He kicked me out, her testy Sire:
And when I stained my hair, that Belle,
Might note the change, and thus admire

And love me, it was sure to dye
A muddy green or staring blue:
Whilst one might trace, with half an eye,
The still triumphant carrot through.

A GAME OF FIVES

Five little girls, of Five, Four, Three, Two, One:
Rolling on the hearthrug, full of tricks and fun.

Five rosy girls, in years from Ten to Six:
Sitting down to lessons—no more time for tricks.

Five growing girls, from Fifteen to Eleven:
Music, Drawing, Languages, and food enough for seven!

Five winsome girls, from Twenty to Sixteen:
Each young man that calls, I say "Now tell me which you mean!"

Five dashing girls, the youngest Twenty-one:
But, if nobody proposes, what is there to be done?

Five showy girls—but Thirty is an age
When girls may be engaging, but they somehow don't engage.

Five dressy girls, of Thirty-one or more:
So gracious to the shy young men they snubbed so much before!

* * * * * *

Five passé girls—Their age? Well, never mind!
We jog along together, like the rest of human kind:
But the quondam "careless bachelor" begins to think he knows
The answer to that ancient problem "how the money goes"!

POETA FIT, NON NASCITUR

"How shall I be a poet?
How shall I write in rhyme?
You told me once 'the very wish
Partook of the sublime.'
Then tell me how! Don't put me off
With your 'another time'!"

The old man smiled to see him,
To hear his sudden sally;
He liked the lad to speak his mind
Enthusiastically;
And thought "There's no hum-drum in him,
Nor any shilly-shally."

"And would you be a poet
Before you've been to school?
Ah, well! I hardly thought you
So absolute a fool.
First learn to be spasmodic—
A very simple rule.

"For first you write a sentence,
And then you chop it small;
Then mix the bits, and sort them out
Just as they chance to fall:
The order of the phrases makes
No difference at all.

"Then, if you'd be impressive,
Remember what I say,
That abstract qualities begin
With capitals alway:

The True, the Good, the Beautiful—
Those are the things that pay!

"Next, when you are describing
A shape, or sound, or tint;
Don't state the matter plainly,
But put it in a hint;
And learn to look at all things
With a sort of mental squint."

"For instance, if I wished, Sir,
Of mutton-pies to tell,
Should I say 'dreams of fleecy flocks
Pent in a wheaten cell'?"
"Why, yes," the old man said: "that phrase
Would answer very well.

"Then fourthly, there are epithets
That suit with any word—
As well as Harvey's Reading Sauce
With fish, or flesh, or bird—
Of these, 'wild,' 'lonely,' 'weary,' 'strange,'
Are much to be preferred."

"And will it do, O will it do
To take them in a lump—
As 'the wild man went his weary way
To a strange and lonely pump'?"
"Nay, nay! You must not hastily
To such conclusions jump.

"Such epithets, like pepper,
Give zest to what you write;
And, if you strew them sparely,
They whet the appetite:

But if you lay them on too thick,
You spoil the matter quite!

"Last, as to the arrangement:
Your reader, you should show him,
Must take what information he
Can get, and look for no im-
mature disclosure of the drift
And purpose of your poem.

"Therefore, to test his patience—
How much he can endure—
Mention no places, names, or dates,
And evermore be sure
Throughout the poem to be found
Consistently obscure.

"First fix upon the limit
To which it shall extend:
Then fill it up with 'Padding'
(Beg some of any friend):
Your great Sensation-stanza
You place towards the end."

"And what is a Sensation,
Grandfather, tell me, pray?
I think I never heard the word
So used before to-day:
Be kind enough to mention one
'Exempli gratiâ.'"

And the old man, looking sadly
Across the garden-lawn,
Where here and there a dew-drop
Yet glittered in the dawn,

Said "Go to the Adelphi,
And see the 'Colleen Bawn.'

"The word is due to Boucicault—
The theory is his,
Where Life becomes a Spasm,
And History a Whiz:
If that is not Sensation,
I don't know what it is.

"Now try your hand, ere Fancy
Have lost its present glow—"
"And then," his grandson added,
"We'll publish it, you know:
Green cloth—gold-lettered at the back—
In duodecimo!"

Then proudly smiled that old man
To see the eager lad
Rush madly for his pen and ink
And for his blotting-pad—
But, when he thought of publishing,
His face grew stern and sad.

THE HUNTING OF THE SNARK,

An Agony in Eight Fits

PREFACE

If—and the thing is wildly possible—the charge of writing nonsense were ever brought against the author of this brief but instructive poem, it would be based, I feel convinced, on the line (in p. 144)

"Then the bowsprit got mixed with the rudder sometimes:"

In view of this painful possibility, I will not (as I might) appeal indignantly to my other writings as a proof that I am incapable of such a deed: I will not (as I might) point to the strong moral purpose of this poem itself, to the arithmetical principles so cautiously inculcated in it, or to its noble teachings in Natural History—I will take the more prosaic course of simply explaining how it happened.

The Bellman, who was almost morbidly sensitive about appearances, used to have the bowsprit unshipped once or twice a week to be revarnished; and it more than once happened, when the time came for replacing it, that no one on board could remember which end of the ship it belonged to. They knew it was not of the slightest use to appeal to the Bellman about it—he would only refer to his Naval Code, and read out in pathetic tones Admiralty Instructions which none of them had ever been able to understand—so it generally ended in its being fastened on, anyhow, across the rudder. The helmsman[1] used to stand by with

---

[1] This office was usually undertaken by the Boots, who found in it a refuge from the Baker's constant complaints about the insufficient blacking of his three pair of boots.

tears in his eyes: he knew it was all wrong, but alas! Rule 42 of the Code, "No one shall speak to the Man at the Helm," had been completed by the Bellman himself with the words "and the Man at the Helm shall speak to no one." So remonstrance was impossible, and no steering could be done till the next varnishing day. During these bewildering intervals the ship usually sailed backwards.

As this poem is to some extent connected with the lay of the Jabberwock, let me take this opportunity of answering a question that has often been asked me, how to pronounce "slithy toves." The "i" in "slithy" is long, as in "writhe"; and "toves" is pronounced so as to rhyme with "groves." Again, the first "o" in "borogoves" is pronounced like the "o" in "borrow." I have heard people try to give it the sound of the "o" in "worry." Such is Human Perversity.

This also seems a fitting occasion to notice the other hard words in that poem. Humpty-Dumpty's theory, of two meanings packed into one word like a portmanteau, seems to me the right explanation for all.

For instance, take the two words "fuming" and "furious." Make up your mind that you will say both words, but leave it unsettled which you will say first. Now open your mouth and speak. If your thoughts incline ever so little towards "fuming," you will say "fuming-furious"; if they turn, by even a hair's breadth towards "furious," you will say "furious-fuming"; but if you have that rarest of gifts, a perfectly balanced mind, you will say "frumious."

Supposing that, when Pistol uttered the well-known words—

"Under which king, Bezonian? Speak or die!"

Justice Shallow had felt certain that it was either William or Richard, but had not been able to settle which, so that he could not possibly say either name before the other, can it be doubted that, rather than die, he would have gasped out "Rilchiam!"

Fit the First

THE LANDING

"Just the place for a Snark!" the Bellman cried,
    As he landed his crew with care;
Supporting each man on the top of the tide
    By a finger entwined in his hair.

"Just the place for a Snark! I have said it twice:
    That alone should encourage the crew.
Just the place for a Snark! I have said it thrice:
    What I tell you three times is true."

The crew was complete: it included a Boots—
    A maker of Bonnets and Hoods—
A Barrister, brought to arrange their disputes—
    And a Broker, to value their goods.

A Billiard-marker, whose skill was immense,
    Might perhaps have won more than his share—
But a Banker, engaged at enormous expense,
    Had the whole of their cash in his care.

There was also a Beaver, that paced on the deck,
    Or would sit making lace in the bow:
And had often (the Bellman said) saved them from wreck,
    Though none of the sailors knew how.

There was one who was famed for the number of things
    He forgot when he entered the ship:
His umbrella, his watch, all his jewels and rings,
    And the clothes he had bought for the trip.

He had forty-two boxes, all carefully packed,
　　With his name painted clearly on each:
But since he omitted to mention the fact,
　　They were all left behind on the beach.

The loss of his clothes hardly mattered, because
　　He had seven coats on when he came,
With three pair of boots—but the worst of it was
　　He had wholly forgotten his name.

He would answer to "Hi!" or to any loud cry,
　　Such as "Fry me!" or "Fritter my wig!"
To "What-you-may-call-um!" or "What-was-his-name!"
　　But especially "Thing-um-a jig!"

While, for those who preferred a more forcible word,
　　He had different names from these:
His intimate friends called him "Candle-ends,"
　　And his enemies "Toasted-cheese."

"His form is ungainly—his intellect small—"
　　(So the Bellman would often remark)—
"But his courage is perfect! And that, after all,
　　Is the thing that one needs with a Snark."

He would joke with hyænas, returning their stare
　　With an impudent wag of the head:
And he once went a walk, paw-in-paw, with a bear,
　　"Just to keep up its spirits," he said.

He came as a Baker: but owned, when too late—
　　And it drove the poor Bellman half-mad—
He could only bake Bride-cake—for which, I may state,
　　No materials were to be had.

The last of the crew needs especial remark,
Though he looked an incredible dunce:
He had just one idea—but, that one being "Snark,"
The good Bellman engaged him at once.

He came as a Butcher: but gravely declared,
When the ship had been sailing a week,
He could only kill Beavers. The Bellman looked scared,
And was almost too frightened to speak:

But at length he explained, in a tremulous tone,
There was only one Beaver on board;
And that was a tame one he had of his own,
Whose death would be deeply deplored.

The Beaver, who happened to hear the remark,
Protested, with tears in its eyes,
That not even the rapture of hunting the Snark
Could atone for that dismal surprise!

It strongly advised that the Butcher should be
Conveyed in a separate ship:
But the Bellman declared that would never agree
With the plans he had made for the trip:

Navigation was always a difficult art,
Though with only one ship and one bell:
And he feared he must really decline, for his part,
Undertaking another as well.

The Beaver's best course was, no doubt, to procure
A second-hand dagger-proof coat—
So the Baker advised it—and next, to insure
Its life in some Office of note:

This the Banker suggested, and offered for hire
(On moderate terms), or for sale,
Two excellent Policies, one Against Fire,
And one Against Damage From Hail.

Yet still, ever after that sorrowful day,
Whenever the Butcher was by,
The Beaver kept looking the opposite way,
And appeared unaccountably shy.

Fit the Second

THE BELLMAN'S SPEECH

The Bellman himself they all praised to the skies—
Such a carriage, such ease and such grace!
Such solemnity, too! One could see he was wise,
The moment one looked in his face!

He had bought a large map representing the sea,
Without the least vestige of land:
And the crew were much pleased when they found it to be
A map they could all understand.

"What's the good of Mercator's North Poles and Equators,
Tropics, Zones, and Meridian Lines?"
So the Bellman would cry: and the crew would reply
"They are merely conventional signs!

"Other maps are such shapes, with their islands and capes!
But we've got our brave Captain to thank"
(So the crew would protest) "that he's bought us the best—
A perfect and absolute blank!"

This was charming, no doubt: but they shortly found out
That the Captain they trusted so well
Had only one notion for crossing the ocean,
And that was to tingle his bell.

He was thoughtful and grave—but the orders he gave
Were enough to bewilder a crew.
When he cried "Steer to starboard, but keep her head larboard!"
What on earth was the helmsman to do?

Then the bowsprit got mixed with the rudder sometimes:
  A thing, as the Bellman remarked,
That frequently happens in tropical climes,
  When a vessel is, so to speak, "snarked."

But the principal failing occurred in the sailing,
  And the Bellman, perplexed and distressed,
Said he had hoped, at least, when the wind blew due East,
  That the ship would not travel due West!

But the danger was past—they had landed at last,
  With their boxes, portmanteaus, and bags:
Yet at first sight the crew were not pleased with the view
  Which consisted of chasms and crags.

The Bellman perceived that their spirits were low,
  And repeated in musical tone
Some jokes he had kept for a season of woe—
  But the crew would do nothing but groan.

He served out some grog with a liberal hand,
  And bade them sit down on the beach:
And they could not but own that their Captain looked grand,
  As he stood and delivered his speech.

"Friends, Romans, and countrymen, lend me your ears!
  (They were all of them fond of quotations:
So they drank to his health, and they gave him three cheers
  While he served out additional rations).

"We have sailed many months, we have sailed many weeks,
  (Four weeks to the month you may mark),
But never as yet ('tis your Captain who speaks)
  Have we caught the least glimpse of a Snark!

"We have sailed many weeks, we have sailed many days,
  (Seven days to the week I allow),
But a Snark, on the which we might lovingly gaze,
  We have never beheld till now!

"Come, listen, my men, while I tell you again
  The five unmistakable marks
By which you may know, wheresoever you go,
  The warranted genuine Snarks.

"Let us take them in order. The first is the taste,
  Which is meagre and hollow, but crisp:
Like a coat that is rather too tight in the waist,
  With a flavour of Will-o-the wisp.

"Its habit of getting up late you'll agree
  That it carries too far, when I say
That it frequently breakfasts at five o'clock tea,
  And dines on the following day.

"The third is its slowness in taking a jest.
  Should you happen to venture on one,
It will sigh like a thing that is deeply distressed:
  And it always looks grave at a pun.

"The fourth is its fondness for bathing-machines,
  Which it constantly carries about,
And believes that they add to the beauty of scenes—
  A sentiment open to doubt.

"The fifth is ambition. It next will be right
  To describe each particular batch:
Distinguishing those that have feathers, and bite,
  From those that have whiskers, and scratch.

"For, although common Snarks do no manner of harm,
　　Yet I feel it my duty to say
Some are Boojums—" The Bellman broke off in alarm,
　　For the Baker had fainted away.

Fit the Third

THE BAKER'S TALE

They roused him with muffins—they roused him with ice—
　　They roused him with mustard and cress—
They roused him with jam and judicious advice—
　　They set him conundrums to guess.

When at length he sat up and was able to speak,
　　His sad story he offered to tell;
And the Bellman cried "Silence! Not even a shriek!"
　　And excitedly tingled his bell.

There was silence supreme! Not a shriek, not a scream;
　　Scarcely even a howl or a groan,
As the man they called "Ho!" told his story of woe
　　In an antediluvian tone.

"My father and mother were honest, though poor—"
　　"Skip all that!" cried the Bellman in haste.
"If it once becomes dark, there's no chance of a Snark—
　　We have hardly a minute to waste!"

"I skip forty years," said the Baker, in tears,
　　"And proceed without further remark
To the day when you took me aboard of your ship
　　To help you in hunting the Snark.

"A dear uncle of mine (after whom I was named)
　　Remarked, when I bade him farewell—"
"Oh, skip your dear uncle!" the Bellman exclaimed,
　　As he angrily tingled his bell.

"He remarked to me then," said that mildest of men,
"'If your Snark be a Snark, that is right:
Fetch it home by all means—you may serve it with greens
And it's handy for striking a light.

"'You may seek it with thimbles—and seek it with care;
You may hunt it with forks and hope;
You may threaten its life with a railway-share;
You may charm it with smiles and soap—'"

("That's exactly the method," the Bellman bold
In a hasty parenthesis cried,
"That's exactly the way I have always been told
That the capture of Snarks should be tried!")

"'But oh, beamish nephew, beware of the day,
If your Snark be a Boojum! For then
You will softly and suddenly vanish away,
And never be met with again!'

"It is this, it is this that oppresses my soul,
When I think of my uncle's last words:
And my heart is like nothing so much as a bowl
Brimming over with quivering curds!

"It is this, it is this—" "We have had that before!"
The Bellman indignantly said.
And the Baker replied "Let me say it once more.
It is this, it is this that I dread!

"I engage with the Snark—every night after dark—
In a dreamy delirious fight:
I serve it with greens in those shadowy scenes,
And I use it for striking a light:

"But if ever I meet with a Boojum, that day,
　In a moment (of this I am sure),
I shall softly and suddenly vanish away—
　And the notion I cannot endure!"

Fit the Fourth

THE HUNTING

The Bellman looked uffish, and wrinkled his brow.
"If only you'd spoken before!
It's excessively awkward to mention it now,
With the Snark, so to speak, at the door!

"We should all of us grieve, as you well may believe,
If you never were met with again—
But surely, my man, when the voyage began,
You might have suggested it then?

"It's excessively awkward to mention it now—
As I think I've already remarked."
And the man they called "Hi!" replied, with a sigh,
"I informed you the day we embarked.

"You may charge me with murder—or want of sense—
(We are all of us weak at times):
But the slightest approach to a false pretence
Was never among my crimes!

"I said it in Hebrew—I said it in Dutch—
I said it in German and Greek:
But I wholly forgot (and it vexes me much)
That English is what you speak!"

"'Tis a pitiful tale," said the Bellman, whose face
Had grown longer at every word:
"But, now that you've stated the whole of your case,
More debate would be simply absurd.

"The rest of my speech" (he explained to his men)
"You shall hear when I've leisure to speak it.
But the Snark is at hand, let me tell you again!
'Tis your glorious duty to seek it!

"To seek it with thimbles, to seek it with care;
To pursue it with forks and hope;
To threaten its life with a railway-share;
To charm it with smiles and soap!

"For the Snark's a peculiar creature, that won't
Be caught in a commonplace way.
Do all that you know, and try all that you don't:
Not a chance must be wasted to-day!

"For England expects—I forbear to proceed:
'Tis a maxim tremendous, but trite:
And you'd best be unpacking the things that you need
To rig yourselves out for the fight."

Then the Banker endorsed a blank cheque (which he crossed),
And changed his loose silver for notes:
The Baker with care combed his whiskers and hair,
And shook the dust out of his coats:

The Boots and the Broker were sharpening a spade—
Each working the grindstone in turn:
But the Beaver went on making lace, and displayed
No interest in the concern:

Though the Barrister tried to appeal to its pride,
And vainly proceeded to cite
A number of cases, in which making laces
Had been proved an infringement of right.

The maker of Bonnets ferociously planned
  A novel arrangement of bows:
While the Billiard-marker with quivering hand
  Was chalking the tip of his nose.

But the Butcher turned nervous, and dressed himself fine,
  With yellow kid gloves and a ruff—
Said he felt it exactly like going to dine,
  Which the Bellman declared was all "stuff."

"Introduce me, now there's a good fellow," he said,
  "If we happen to meet it together!"
And the Bellman, sagaciously nodding his head,
  Said "That must depend on the weather."

The Beaver went simply galumphing about,
  At seeing the Butcher so shy:
And even the Baker, though stupid and stout,
  Made an effort to wink with one eye.

"Be a man!" cried the Bellman in wrath, as he heard
  The Butcher beginning to sob.
"Should we meet with a Jubjub, that desperate bird,
  We shall need all our strength for the job!"

Fit the Fifth

THE BEAVER'S LESSON

They sought it with thimbles, they sought it with care
They pursued it with forks and hope;
They threatened its life with a railway-share;
They charmed it with smiles and soap.

Then the Butcher contrived an ingenious plan
For making a separate sally;
And had fixed on a spot unfrequented by man,
A dismal and desolate valley.

But the very same plan to the Beaver occurred:
It had chosen the very same place:
Yet neither betrayed, by a sign or a word,
The disgust that appeared in his face.

Each thought he was thinking of nothing but "Snark"
And the glorious work of the day;
And each tried to pretend that he did not remark
That the other was going that way.

But the valley grew narrow and narrower still,
And the evening got darker and colder,
Till (merely from nervousness, not from good will)
They marched along shoulder to shoulder.

Then a scream, shrill and high, rent the shuddering sky,
And they knew that some danger was near:
The Beaver turned pale to the tip of its tail,
And even the Butcher felt queer.

He thought of his childhood, left far far behind —
That blissful and innocent state —
The sound so exactly recalled to his mind
A pencil that squeaks on a slate!

"'Tis the voice of the Jubjub!" he suddenly cried.
(This man, that they used to call "Dunce.")
"As the Bellman would tell you," he added with pride,
"I have uttered that sentiment once."

"'Tis the note of the Jubjub! Keep count, I entreat;
You will find I have told it you twice.
'Tis the song of the Jubjub! The proof is complete,
If only I've stated it thrice."

The Beaver had counted with scrupulous care,
Attending to every word:
But it fairly lost heart, and outgrabe in despair,
When the third repetition occurred.

It felt that, in spite of all possible pains,
It had somehow contrived to lose count,
And the only thing now was to rack its poor brains
By reckoning up the amount.

"Two added to one — if that could but be done,"
It said, "with one's fingers and thumbs!"
Recollecting with tears how, in earlier years,
It had taken no pains with its sums.

"The thing can be done," said the Butcher, "I think.
The thing must be done, I am sure.
The thing shall be done! Bring me paper and ink,
The best there is time to procure."

The Beaver brought paper, portfolio, pens,
And ink in unfailing supplies:
While strange creepy creatures came out of their dens,
And watched them with wondering eyes.

So engrossed was the Butcher, he heeded them not,
As he wrote with a pen in each hand,
And explained all the while in a popular style
Which the Beaver could well understand.

"Taking Three as the subject to reason about—
A convenient number to state—
We add Seven, and Ten, and then multiply out
By One Thousand diminished by Eight.

"The result we proceed to divide, as you see,
By Nine-Hundred-and-Ninety-and-Two:
Then subtract Seventeen, and the answer must be
Exactly and perfectly true.

"The method employed I would gladly explain,
While I have it so clear in my head,
If I had but the time and you had but the brain—
But much yet remains to be said.

"In one moment I've seen what has hitherto been
Enveloped in absolute mystery,
And without extra charge I will give you at large
A Lesson in Natural History."

In his genial way he proceeded to say
(Forgetting all laws of propriety,
And that giving instruction, without introduction,
Would have caused quite a thrill in Society),

"As to temper the Jubjub's a desperate bird,
  Since it lives in perpetual passion:
Its taste in costume is entirely absurd—
  It is ages ahead of the fashion:

"But it knows any friend it has met once before:
  It never will look at a bribe:
And in charity-meetings it stands at the door,
  And collects—though it does not subscribe.

"Its flavour when cooked is more exquisite far
  Than mutton, or oysters, or eggs:
(Some think it keeps best in an ivory jar,
  And some, in mahogany kegs:)

"You boil it in sawdust: you salt it in glue:
  You condense it with locusts and tape:
Still keeping one principal object in view—
  To preserve its symmetrical shape."

The Butcher would gladly have talked till next day,
  But he felt that the Lesson must end,
And he wept with delight in attempting to say
  He considered the Beaver his friend:

While the Beaver confessed, with affectionate looks
  More eloquent even than tears,
It had learned in ten minutes far more than all books
  Would have taught it in seventy years.

They returned hand-in-hand, and the Bellman, unmanned
  (For a moment) with noble emotion,
Said "This amply repays all the wearisome days
  We have spent on the billowy ocean!"

Such friends, as the Beaver and Butcher became,
 Have seldom if ever been known;
In winter or summer, 'twas always the same—
 You could never meet either alone.

And when quarrels arose—as one frequently finds
 Quarrels will, spite of every endeavour—
The song of the Jubjub recurred to their minds,
 And cemented their friendship for ever!

Fit the Sixth

THE BARRISTER'S DREAM

They sought it with thimbles, they sought it with care;
    They pursued it with forks and hope;
They threatened its life with a railway-share;
    They charmed it with smiles and soap.

But the Barrister, weary of proving in vain
    That the Beaver's lace-making was wrong,
Fell asleep, and in dreams saw the creature quite plain
    That his fancy had dwelt on so long.

He dreamed that he stood in a shadowy Court,
    Where the Snark, with a glass in its eye,
Dressed in gown, bands, and wig, was defending a pig
    On the charge of deserting its sty.

The Witnesses proved, without error or flaw,
    That the sty was deserted when found:
And the Judge kept explaining the state of the law
    In a soft under-current of sound.

The indictment had never been clearly expressed,
    And it seemed that the Snark had begun,
And had spoken three hours, before any one guessed
    What the pig was supposed to have done.

The Jury had each formed a different view
    (Long before the indictment was read),
And they all spoke at once, so that none of them knew
    One word that the others had said.

"You must know—" said the Judge: but the Snark exclaimed
"Fudge!
That statute is obsolete quite!
Let me tell you, my friends, the whole question depends
On an ancient manorial right.

"In the matter of Treason the pig would appear
To have aided, but scarcely abetted:
While the charge of Insolvency fails, it is clear,
If you grant the plea 'never indebted.'

"The fact of Desertion I will not dispute:
But its guilt, as I trust, is removed
(So far as relates to the costs of this suit)
By the Alibi which has been proved.

"My poor client's fate now depends on your votes."
Here the speaker sat down in his place,
And directed the Judge to refer to his notes
And briefly to sum up the case.

But the Judge said he never had summed up before;
So the Snark undertook it instead,
And summed it so well that it came to far more
Than the Witnesses ever had said!

When the verdict was called for, the Jury declined,
As the word was so puzzling to spell;
But they ventured to hope that the Snark wouldn't mind
Undertaking that duty as well.

So the Snark found the verdict, although, as it owned,
It was spent with the toils of the day:
When it said the word "GUILTY!" the Jury all groaned
And some of them fainted away.

Then the Snark pronounced sentence, the Judge being quite
    Too nervous to utter a word:
When it rose to its feet, there was silence like night,
    And the fall of a pin might be heard.

"Transportation for life" was the sentence it gave,
    "And then to be fined forty pound."
The Jury all cheered, though the Judge said he feared
    That the phrase was not legally sound.

But their wild exultation was suddenly checked
    When the jailer informed them, with tears,
Such a sentence would have not the slightest effect,
    As the pig had been dead for some years.

The Judge left the Court, looking deeply disgusted:
    But the Snark, though a little aghast,
As the lawyer to whom the defence was intrusted,
    Went bellowing on to the last.

Thus the Barrister dreamed, while the bellowing seemed
    To grow every moment more clear:
Till he woke to the knell of a furious bell,
    Which the Bellman rang close at his ear.

Fit the Seventh

THE BANKER'S FATE

They sought it with thimbles, they sought it with care;
They pursued it with forks and hope;
They threatened its life with a railway-share;
They charmed it with smiles and soap.

And the Banker, inspired with a courage so new
It was matter for general remark,
Rushed madly ahead and was lost to their view
In his zeal to discover the Snark.

But while he was seeking with thimbles and care,
A Bandersnatch swiftly drew nigh
And grabbed at the Banker, who shrieked in despair,
For he knew it was useless to fly.

He offered large discount—he offered a cheque
(Drawn "to bearer") for seven-pounds-ten:
But the Bandersnatch merely extended its neck
And grabbed at the Banker again.

Without rest or pause—while those frumious jaws
Went savagely snapping around—
He skipped and he hopped, and he floundered and flopped,
Till fainting he fell to the ground.

The Bandersnatch fled as the others appeared
Led on by that fear-stricken yell:
And the Bellman remarked "It is just as I feared!"
And solemnly tolled on his bell.

He was black in the face, and they scarcely could trace
　　The least likeness to what he had been:
While so great was his fright that his waistcoat turned
　　　　white—
　　A wonderful thing to be seen!

To the horror of all who were present that day,
　　He uprose in full evening dress,
And with senseless grimaces endeavoured to say
　　What his tongue could no longer express.

Down he sank in a chair—ran his hands through his hair—
　　And chanted in mimsiest tones
Words whose utter inanity proved his insanity,
　　While he rattled a couple of bones.

"Leave him here to his fate—it is getting so late!"
　　The Bellman exclaimed in a fright.
"We have lost half the day. Any further delay,
And we sha'n't catch a Snark before night!"

Fit the Eighth

THE VANISHING

They sought it with thimbles, they sought it with care;
   They pursued it with forks and hope;
They threatened its life with a railway-share;
   They charmed it with smiles and soap.

They shuddered to think that the chase might fail,
   And the Beaver, excited at last,
Went bounding along on the tip of its tail,
   For the daylight was nearly past.

"There is Thingumbob shouting!" the Bellman said.
   "He is shouting like mad, only hark!
He is waving his hands, he is wagging his head,
   He has certainly found a Snark!"

They gazed in delight, while the Butcher exclaimed
   "He was always a desperate wag!"
They beheld him—their Baker—their hero unnamed—
   On the top of a neighbouring crag,

Erect and sublime, for one moment of time.
   In the next, that wild figure they saw
(As if stung by a spasm) plunge into a chasm,
   While they waited and listened in awe.

"It's a Snark!" was the sound that first came to their ears,
   And seemed almost too good to be true.
Then followed a torrent of laughter and cheers:
   Then the ominous words "It's a Boo—"

Then, silence. Some fancied they heard in the air
   A weary and wandering sigh
That sounded like "—jum!" but the others declare
   It was only a breeze that went by.

They hunted till darkness came on, but they found
   Not a button, or feather, or mark,
By which they could tell that they stood on the ground
   Where the Baker had met with the Snark.

In the midst of the word he was trying to say,
   In the midst of his laughter and glee,
He had softly and suddenly vanished away—
   For the Snark was a Boojum, you see.

SIZE AND TEARS

When on the sandy shore I sit,
    Beside the salt sea-wave,
And fall into a weeping fit
    Because I dare not shave —
A little whisper at my ear
Enquires the reason of my fear.

I answer "If that ruffian Jones
    Should recognise me here,
He'd bellow out my name in tones
    Offensive to the ear:
He chaffs me so on being stout
(A thing that always puts me out)."

Ah me! I see him on the cliff!
    Farewell, farewell to hope,
If he should look this way, and if
    He's got his telescope!
To whatsoever place I flee,
My odious rival follows me!

For every night, and everywhere,
    I meet him out at dinner;
And when I've found some charming fair,
    And vowed to die or win her,
The wretch (he's thin and I am stout)
Is sure to come and cut me out!

The girls (just like them!) all agree
    To praise J. Jones, Esquire:
I ask them what on earth they see
    About him to admire?

They cry "He is so sleek and slim,
It's quite a treat to look at him!"

They vanish in tobacco smoke,
Those visionary maids—
I feel a sharp and sudden poke
Between the shoulder-blades—
"Why, Brown, my boy! You're growing stout!"
(I told you he would find me out!)

"My growth is not your business, Sir!"
"No more it is, my boy!
But if it's yours, as I infer,
Why, Brown, I give you joy!
A man, whose business prospers so,
Is just the sort of man to know!

"It's hardly safe, though, talking here—
I'd best get out of reach:
For such a weight as yours, I fear,
Must shortly sink the beach!"—
Insult me thus because I'm stout!
I vow I'll go and call him out!

ATALANTA IN CAMDEN-TOWN

Ay, 'twas here, on this spot,
In that summer of yore,
Atalanta did not
Vote my presence a bore,
Nor reply to my tenderest talk "She had heard all that nonsense before."

She'd the brooch I had bought
And the necklace and sash on,
And her heart, as I thought,
Was alive to my passion;
And she'd done up her hair in the style that the Empress had brought into fashion.

I had been to the play
With my pearl of a Peri—
But, for all I could say,
She declared she was weary,
That "the place was so crowded and hot, and she couldn't abide that Dundreary."

Then I thought "'Tis for me
That she whines and she whimpers!"
And it soothed me to see
Those sensational simpers,
And I said "This is scrumptious!"—a phrase I had learned from the Devonshire shrimpers.

And I vowed "'Twill be said
I'm a fortunate fellow,
When the breakfast is spread,
When the topers are mellow,

When the foam of the bride-cake is white, and the fierce orange-
blossoms are yellow!"

O that languishing yawn!
O those eloquent eyes!
I was drunk with the dawn
Of a splendid surmise—
I was stung by a look, I was slain by a tear, by a tempest of sighs.

And I whispered "'Tis time!
Is not Love at its deepest?
Shall we squander Life's prime,
While thou waitest and weepest?
Let us settle it, License or Banns?—though undoubtedly Banns are
the cheapest."

"Ah, my Hero," said I,
"Let me be thy Leander!"
But I lost her reply—
Something ending with "gander"—
For the omnibus rattled so loud that no mortal could quite
understand her.

THE LANG COORTIN'

The ladye she stood at her lattice high,
   Wi' her doggie at her feet;
Thorough the lattice she can spy
   The passers in the street.

"There's one that standeth at the door,
   And tirleth at the pin:
Now speak and say, my popinjay,
   If I sall let him in."

Then up and spake the popinjay
   That flew abune her head:
"Gae let him in that tirls the pin:
   He cometh thee to wed."

O when he cam' the parlour in,
   A woeful man was he!
"And dinna ye ken your lover agen,
   Sae well that loveth thee?"

"And how wad I ken ye loved me, Sir,
   That have been sae lang away?
And how wad I ken ye loved me, Sir?
   Ye never telled me sae."

Said—"Ladye dear," and the salt, salt tear
   Cam' rinnin' doon his cheek,
"I have sent thee tokens of my love
   This many and many a week.

"O didna ye get the rings, Ladye,
   The rings o' the gowd sae fine?

> I wot that I have sent to thee
> Four score, four score and nine."

"They cam' to me," said that fair ladye.
"Wow, they were flimsie things!"
Said—"that chain o' gowd, my doggie to howd,
It is made o' thae self-same rings."

"And didna ye get the locks, the locks,
The locks o' my ain black hair,
Whilk I sent by post, whilk I sent by box,
Whilk I sent by the carrier?"

"They cam' to me," said that fair ladye;
"And I prithee send nae mair!"
Said—"that cushion sae red, for my doggie's head,
It is stuffed wi' thae locks o' hair."

"And didna ye get the letter, Ladye,
Tied wi' a silken string,
Whilk I sent to thee frae the far countrie,
A message of love to bring?"

"It cam' to me frae the far countrie
Wi' its silken string and a';
But it wasna prepaid," said that high-born maid,
"Sae I gar'd them tak' it awa'."

"O ever alack that ye sent it back,
It was written sae clerkly and well!
Now the message it brought, and the boon that it sought,
I must even say it mysel'."

Then up and spake the popinjay,
Sae wisely counselled he.

"Now say it in the proper way:
    Gae doon upon thy knee!"
The lover he turned baith red and pale,
    Went doon upon his knee:
"O Ladye, hear the waesome tale
    That must be told to thee!

"For five lang years, and five lang years,
    I coorted thee by looks;
By nods and winks, by smiles and tears,
    As I had read in books.

"For ten lang years, O weary hours!
    I coorted thee by signs;
By sending game, by sending flowers,
    By sending Valentines.

"For five lang years, and five lang years,
    I have dwelt in the far countrie,
Till that thy mind should be inclined
    Mair tenderly to me.

"Now thirty years are gane and past,
    I am come frae a foreign land:
I am come to tell thee my love at last—
    O Ladye, gie me thy hand!"

The ladye she turned not pale nor red,
    But she smiled a pitiful smile:
"Sic' a coortin' as yours, my man," she said
    "Takes a lang and a weary while!"

And out and laughed the popinjay,
    A laugh of bitter scorn:
"A coortin' done in sic' a way,
    It ought not to be borne!"

Wi' that the doggie barked aloud,
And up and doon he ran,
And tugged and strained his chain o' gowd,
All for to bite the man.

"O hush thee, gentle popinjay!
O hush thee, doggie dear!
There is a word I fain wad say,
It needeth he should hear!"

Aye louder screamed that ladye fair
To drown her doggie's bark:
Ever the lover shouted mair
To make that ladye hark:

Shrill and more shrill the popinjay
Upraised his angry squall:
I trow the doggie's voice that day
Was louder than them all!

The serving-men and serving-maids
Sat by the kitchen fire:
They heard sic' a din the parlour within
As made them much admire.

Out spake the boy in buttons
(I ween he wasna thin),
"Now wha will tae the parlour gae,
And stay this deadlie din?"

And they have taen a kerchief,
Casted their kevils in,
For wha should tae the parlour gae,
And stay that deadlie din.

When on that boy the kevil fell
　　To stay the fearsome noise,
"Gae in," they cried, "whate'er betide,
　　Thou prince of button-boys!"

Syne, he has taen a supple cane
　　To swinge that dog sae fat:
The doggie yowled, the doggie howled
　　The louder aye for that.

Syne, he has taen a mutton-bane—
　　The doggie ceased his noise,
And followed doon the kitchen stair
　　That prince of button-boys!

Then sadly spake that ladye fair,
　　Wi' a frown upon her brow:
"O dearer to me is my sma' doggie
　　Than a dozen sic' as thou!

"Nae use, nae use for sighs and tears:
　　Nae use at all to fret:
Sin' ye've bided sae well for thirty years,
　　Ye may bide a wee langer yet!"

Sadly, sadly he crossed the floor
　　And tirlëd at the pin:
Sadly went he through the door
　　Where sadly he cam' in.

"O gin I had a popinjay
　　To fly abune my head,
To tell me what I ought to say,
　　I had by this been wed.

"O gin I find anither ladye,"
He said wi' sighs and tears,
"I wot my coortin' sall not be
    Anither thirty years:

"For gin I find a ladye gay,
    Exactly to my taste,
I'll pop the question, aye or nay,
    In twenty years at maist."

FOUR RIDDLES

[These consist of two Double Acrostics and two Charades.

No. I. was written at the request of some young friends, who had gone to a ball at an Oxford Commemoration—and also as a specimen of what might be done by making the Double Acrostic a connected poem instead of what it has hitherto been, a string of disjointed stanzas, on every conceivable subject, and about as interesting to read straight through as a page of a Cyclopædia. The first two stanzas describe the two main words, and each subsequent stanza one of the cross "lights."

No. II. was written after seeing Miss Ellen Terry perform in the play of "Hamlet." In this case the first stanza describes the two main words.

No. III. was written after seeing Miss Marion Terry perform in Mr. Gilbert's play of "Pygmalion and Galatea." The three stanzas respectively describe "My First," "My Second," and "My Whole."

I

There was an ancient City, stricken down
With a strange frenzy, and for many a day
They paced from morn to eve the crowded town,
    And danced the night away.

I asked the cause: the aged man grew sad:
They pointed to a building gray and tall,
And hoarsely answered "Step inside, my lad,
    And then you'll see it all."

Yet what are all such gaieties to me
Whose thoughts are full of indices and surds?
$x^2 + 7x + 53$
    $= 11/3$.

But something whispered "It will soon be done:
Bands cannot always play, nor ladies smile:
Endure with patience the distasteful fun
   For just a little while!"

A change came o'er my Vision—it was night:
We clove a pathway through a frantic throng:
The steeds, wild-plunging, filled us with affright:
   The chariots whirled along.

Within a marble hall a river ran—
A living tide, half muslin and half cloth:
And here one mourned a broken wreath or fan,
   Yet swallowed down her wrath;

And here one offered to a thirsty fair
(His words half-drowned amid those thunders tuneful)
Some frozen viand (there were many there),
   A tooth-ache in each spoonful.

There comes a happy pause, for human strength
Will not endure to dance without cessation;
And every one must reach the point at length
   Of absolute prostration.

At such a moment ladies learn to give,
To partners who would urge them over-much,
A flat and yet decided negative—
   Photographers love such.

There comes a welcome summons—hope revives,
And fading eyes grow bright, and pulses quicken:
Incessant pop the corks, and busy knives
   Dispense the tongue and chicken.

Flushed with new life, the crowd flows back again:
And all is tangled talk and mazy motion—
Much like a waving field of golden grain,
        Or a tempestuous ocean.

And thus they give the time, that Nature meant
For peaceful sleep and meditative snores,
To ceaseless din and mindless merriment
        And waste of shoes and floors.

And One (we name him not) that flies the flowers,
That dreads the dances, and that shuns the salads,
They doom to pass in solitude the hours,
        Writing acrostic-ballads.

How late it grows! The hour is surely past
That should have warned us with its double-knock?
The twilight wanes, and morning comes at last—
        "Oh, Uncle, what's o'clock?"

The Uncle gravely nods, and wisely winks.
It may mean much, but how is one to know?
He opes his mouth—yet out of it, methinks,
        No words of wisdom flow.

II

    Empress of Art, for thee I twine
This wreath with all too slender skill.
Forgive my Muse each halting line,
    And for the deed accept the will!

O day of tears! Whence comes this spectre grim,
Parting, like Death's cold river, souls that love?

Is not he bound to thee, as thou to him,
By vows, unwhispered here, yet heard above?

And still it lives, that keen and heavenward flame,
Lives in his eye, and trembles in his tone:
And these wild words of fury but proclaim
A heart that beats for thee, for thee alone!

But all is lost: that mighty mind o'erthrown,
Like sweet bells jangled, piteous sight to see!
"Doubt that the stars are fire," so runs his moan,
"Doubt Truth herself, but not my love for thee!"

A sadder vision yet: thine aged sire
Shaming his hoary locks with treacherous wile!
And dost thou now doubt Truth to be a liar?
And wilt thou die, that hast forgot to smile?

Nay, get thee hence! Leave all thy winsome ways
And the faint fragrance of thy scattered flowers:
In holy silence wait the appointed days,
And weep away the leaden-footed hours.

III

The air is bright with hues of light
And rich with laughter and with singing:
Young hearts beat high in ecstasy,
And banners wave, and bells are ringing:
But silence falls with fading day,
And there's an end to mirth and play.
Ah, well-a-day!

Rest your old bones, ye wrinkled crones!
The kettle sings, the firelight dances.

Deep be it quaffed, the magic draught
That fills the soul with golden fancies!
For Youth and Pleasure will not stay,
And ye are withered, worn, and gray.
  Ah, well-a-day!

O fair cold face! O form of grace,
For human passion madly yearning!
O weary air of dumb despair,
From marble won, to marble turning!
"Leave us not thus!" we fondly pray.
"We cannot let thee pass away!"
  Ah, well-a-day!

IV

My First is singular at best:
More plural is my Second:
My Third is far the pluralest—
So plural-plural, I protest
  It scarcely can be reckoned!

My First is followed by a bird:
My Second by believers
In magic art: my simple Third
Follows, too often, hopes absurd
  And plausible deceivers.

My First to get at wisdom tries—
A failure melancholy!
My Second men revered as wise:
My Third from heights of wisdom flies
  To depths of frantic folly.

My First is ageing day by day:

My Second's age is ended:
My Third enjoys an age, they say,
That never seems to fade away,
Through centuries extended.

My Whole? I need a poet's pen
To paint her myriad phases:
The monarch, and the slave, of men—
A mountain-summit, and a den
Of dark and deadly mazes—

A flashing light—a fleeting shade—
Beginning, end, and middle
Of all that human art hath made
Or wit devised! Go, seek her aid,
If you would read my riddle!

FAME'S PENNY-TRUMPET

[Affectionately dedicated to all "original researchers" who pant for "endowment."]

Blow, blow your trumpets till they crack,
Ye little men of little souls!
And bid them huddle at your back—
Gold-sucking leeches, shoals on shoals!

Fill all the air with hungry wails—
"Reward us, ere we think or write!
Without your Gold mere Knowledge fails
To sate the swinish appetite!"

And, where great Plato paced serene,
Or Newton paused with wistful eye,
Rush to the chace with hoofs unclean
And Babel-clamour of the sty!

Be yours the pay: be theirs the praise:
We will not rob them of their due,
Nor vex the ghosts of other days
By naming them along with you.

They sought and found undying fame:
They toiled not for reward nor thanks:
Their cheeks are hot with honest shame
For you, the modern mountebanks!

Who preach of Justice—plead with tears
That Love and Mercy should abound—
While marking with complacent ears
The moaning of some tortured hound:

Who prate of Wisdom—nay, forbear,
　Lest Wisdom turn on you in wrath,
Trampling, with heel that will not spare,
　The vermin that beset her path!

Go, throng each other's drawing-rooms,
　Ye idols of a petty clique:
Strut your brief hour in borrowed plumes,
　And make your penny-trumpets squeak:

Deck your dull talk with pilfered shreds
　Of learning from a nobler time,
And oil each other's little heads
　With mutual Flattery's golden slime:

And when the topmost height ye gain,
　And stand in Glory's ether clear,
And grasp the prize of all your pain—
　So many hundred pounds a year—

Then let Fame's banner be unfurled!
　Sing Pæans for a victory won!
Ye tapers, that would light the world,
　And cast a shadow on the Sun—

Who still shall pour His rays sublime,
　One crystal flood, from East to West,
When ye have burned your little time
　And feebly flickered into rest!

THE END

www.ingramcontent.com/pod-product-compliance
Lightning Source LLC
Chambersburg PA
CBHW011256040426
42453CB00015B/2425